DIVA, LLC.

Diary of a DIVA

Autobiographical Poetry and Politically Incorrect Statements

authorHOUSE®

AuthorHouse™
1663 Liberty Drive
Bloomington, IN 47403
www.authorhouse.com
Phone: 1-800-839-8640

Published by AuthorHouse 5/29/2013

ISBN: 978-1-4520-8917-1 (sc)
ISBN: 978-1-4520-9492-2 (hc)
ISBN: 978-1-4520-8918-8 (e)

Dedication

For my daughters Katana and Kyetra, the world is yours. Conquer.

For Pat Gage, my classmate who wrote on my title page,
"Yvette, you do not have to apologize for your reality."

For Michael, through your gifts you gave me the courage to
sing and write without fear. Rest in peace. I miss you.

For Aunt Millie, I've always referred to you as my angel.
Now you have your wings. Thank you for your wisdom,
love, humor, and patience. Please continue to wrap your
spirit around us. I miss you so much. Rest in peace.

Daddy, mission accomplished.

Thank you...

Kelly Mitchell- graphic designer, illustrator

Mitchell Stanford- photographer, graphic designer

Moses Montgomery- CD producer and engineer

Joe Winner- CD engineer

Logan Queen-photographer

Dr. Jon Saari- graduate creative writing advisor

Dr. Marge Mott- graduate creative writing professor

Tim and Linda Potter, school of advertising
art founders- supporters

Tom Martino- mentor

Judith Chandler- undying support

Muevelo Diva family and supporters

My heavenly Father, I thank you for your grace, love, and patience

for I *know*

I am a handful.

Disclaimer

These are my words

My words are my life

I bleed through my words

If you don't understand you are too young

If my words offend you are too old

I spare no feelings-mine have not been

I love

Hate

Rejoice

Grieve

Bleed.

If I make you feel what I want you to feel then I've done my job

These are my words

My dance, my song, my rhythm

I give them to you

To smile, laugh, cry, think, relate

To heal.

Take them…and take heed.

Drummer Girl

I feel I'm a person of reasonable character.

I work, I dream, I love, I get pissed off,

I'm addicted to nothing, I get naturally high, I admit my wrongs,

I give no excuses.

Wherever I go I leave my mark.

Whatever I do I make a statement

Whatever I say I give a message.

I am rarely in fashion…but always in style.

I can hear you and not listen,

      speak to you and not see you

      fuck a man and not love him.

I march to the beat of a different drum

And I bang my own damn drum.

July 7, 2009

My dearest love,

On June 25th 2009 at 2:26 PM Pacific time, my heart stopped momentarily. It stopped with yours.

When you entered my life in 1974, I knew our bond would be eternal. Over the years you made me smile, blush, scream, cry, dance, but most importantly you told me to sing.

So I did.

You gave me a beat, taught me riffs, and gave me the courage to adlib without fear. You gave my voice a song and I sang with you. Hours upon hours I sang with you and mimicked your style while developing my own. You were there. My hero, my music, and my first love.

I leaned on you through my teen years as a source of strength to keep on singing when life was taking its dreadful courses and painful life lessons were learned. I was able to hold onto you and the melody you gave me.

Then came the media.

You went through so many changes, the nose, the hair, the lips, and it never fazed me. As long as I was able to read your eyes and hear your voice, there was nothing you could to your exterior that could possibly affect your interior or my unconditional love for you. You always remained real to me. My hero, my music, and my first love.

Growing up I always had it in my heart that I was to be Mrs. Michael Jackson. No young lady loved you more than I did. No one had your back like I did. When the kids made fun, I fought. When the media talked trash, I talked trash back. I became your media assassin while I was a member of the media. Regardless of how your look evolved, you were always the man I loved who put the music in me.

Then came the other women.

I understood that they were celebrities and lived the rigorous lifestyle that you were accustomed to. But know that I understood also and I had your back the entire time and I waited for you to come to me…like every other girl in the world. I just thought I was different and I was correct.

I am different because you made me different.

I am watching your memorial service denial. A part of my being was taken with you as you formed your new body with God. I just wish we had more time. Today I am overcome with survivor's guilt. I am broken. I feel so lost without you. However, I accept that your new form is divine and I'm working to be at peace and it hasn't been easy.

Today I am referred to as a "die-hard." I find that interesting. The same attitude and love I have for you now, is the same love and attitude I've had since 1974. So be it. As always, I have no shame in expressing my love and appreciation for you. After all, you have been my man for over thirty years. I am receiving strange looks, folks referring to me as crazy, laughing at me, shaking their heads, and probably wondering why it is that I am so broken. It remains as it has always been with you and I- none of anyone's concern if they don't understand.

Please forgive me for my selfishness. While all I have spoken of is myself and how your loss has affected me, I can't even fathom the pain that your family is enduring. Trust that I will keep them all in prayer.

I'm trying to wrap this up but it is so difficult for me to say goodbye to you. Guilt sets in as I recall how you were my entire childhood, yet you never had one. Thank you for love, thank you for my voice, and thank you for showing me that I am able to touch and heal through music. Thank you for your smile, your compassion, that moonwalk, the glitter, and your dominant presence. Thank you for allowing me to look into your eyes.

Our heavenly Father has an amazing plan for you now. Goodness, I can't imagine you topping what you've accomplished down here, but baby I gotta tell you what makes me sick is the same deceitful people who called you "wacko" as recently as last week, praise your name today. These are the same self-serving, self gratifying, two-faced bastards who worked tirelessly to deface, demean, defeat, and destroy you. Will they leave you alone now? Will you rest in peace rather than rest in pieces?

I am proud to have your music and your influence melodically running intravenously. I miss you and I am with you for eternity. To simply say that I love you is such a gross, insulting understatement so I'll end with...

Until we meet again Michael. You will always remain my King and the music in me.

Your girl,
Yvette

They say the Lord giveth and taketh away.
I receiveth and flushed it.

D'Ciara? Elishah?

It was so small.
Just a tiny figure…   in the toilet

Sort of makes one scared to pee when you're pregnant
…wondering what the hell will fall out next.

I flushed my baby down the toilet tonight.
Was that a pro-life or pro-choice decision?

I hurt - everywhere
Like someone ran a truck through my ass.

I believe life starts at conception.
It ended in the toilet.

I heard "mommy" as I watched my baby go under.

I cried "baby" as I went along.

Allegiance (age 19)

In my New York elementary school
I was made to recite the pledge of allegiance
And sing the National Anthem
It wasn't a problem for me

Back then

But things are different
Times have changed
I've grown up

"Oh say does that star-spangled banner yet wave...
Ore the land of the...

What is free?

Webster's dictionary defines "free" as enjoying civil and political liberty
not subject to the control or domination of another.

Again.

What the hell is free?

Let's talk about this definition
"Not subject to the control or domination of another"
That ranks right up there with "liberty and justice for all."

Those who had liberty and justice from the get go
Are STILL fighting to get just some of their land back to which
they were indigenous
Don't forget indigenous means NATIVE

And even the term "native" makes me giggle because these people were kicked off and killed off their land.

...with liberty and justice for who?

This is their land. They are our founding fathers.

Yet we still celebrate ignorance (and honor a holiday) in the form of a man who claimed
"I discovered you...I found you."

Response:

"You did not discover nor did you find shit because my people were never lost."
How can one discover those who were civilized and practiced democracy BEFORE you arrived?

This is stupid to me.

Unless you are a Native American
We are living on land which is not ours
With a leader who ain't no more Native than we are
Trying to live up to the name we gave ourselves
We pledge allegiance to a flag instead of a God
We need authorization from a government (another group of non-Natives) to leave this land and return to it

And the Natives...please.

Correct me if I am wrong
Isn't America all about "liberty and justice for all"
not just for some
"not subject to the domination of another"

Let me state for the record-
I choose no other place to live than the United States of America
but
This patriotic fantasy, and the the perpetuation of ignorance has
got to stop

I still sing America
I always will
And it still hurts
Just please remember, there is no holiday, while celebrating murder
and genocide

So please don't condemn me when you see me down praying
rather than standing with you
Lying
in tears
With one hand

Under God

...invisible...

Katana

My heroine

Protection from all that is wrong

I strive to have your heart, your sensitive soul

You are grace, kindness and generosity

Until crossed

My guardian angel

May your wingspan know no boundaries

Yvette Williams

Kyetra

You are regal

My Queen

Your strength, your spirit- are admirable

Your determination to do

Your courage to be

Through your eyes I view my soul

I am proud to be of you

Deadbeat dad

Sorry, spineless, simple

How could you not care?

One has your smile

The other your eyes

They are beautiful

What is your issue?

Doped up, slouching,

Such a display of cowardice and

Dumb as a box of rocks

Dude, wipe that goofy fucking smile off your face…

WAIT…

Why am I wasting my words on such an unworthy being?

…next page please…

For My Girls

My desire

was giving you everything I could

That was my first mistake.

I worked so hard,

Taking jobs I had no business taking

Working crazy hours

Graveyard combo shifts and all

I was so wrapped up in a larger paycheck,

a nicer home, a newer car, Toys R us, ballet and gymnastics

lessons, your hair,

and the news that I almost forgot to give you myself.

You know the simple stuff I miss like singing to you,

rubbing your back until you fall asleep

and our family prayer

So if I may...

I'd like to start fresh (I won't say start over because those labor

pains were a mutha)

But sorta pick up where I left off before I got so caught up

…in what never really mattered.

For My Boy

I feel as if I let you down

You trusted me

And my commitment to you

This melancholy travels through my being like a ravenous cancer

Uncontrolled

Relentless pain

I wish I could have taken it for you

I'm almost envious

You were my boy

I'll cherish singing to you

While you closed your big brown eyes in my arms

Our love was happy, unique, Divine, sent

An attempted explanation would simply minimize its value

Forever my boy

As you take on your new body with God

The bond we have will never be broken

Rest in peace my Prince

Mommy June 8, 2004

On Blackness

Beauty is my child

I bathed it saved it and raised it

To be like me

I am beauty

My beauty ain't skin deep

It's skin surface

Dark, rich, majestic

My beauty has tone

Not "Coppertone"

Natural tone

Ebony, honey, mahogany

Yes, I'm proud of my child

My gift

My creation

My beauty

(1986)

It's the kind of stuff you hide or simply don't tell others (especially your kids) because

you just don't want to share.

It's insane.

I portioned it out just enough to last me for another 3 meals before I faced that I would

have to go back groveling with an empty bowl for more.

This stuff was amazing. I mean really good.

Chock full of color, flavor, texture, without being calorically sinful -if that is even a

word- but I hid it eating it only after 1am when I knew I could be alone to enjoy this gift.

No one could taste.

Cause they would love it and I'd never see my bowl again.

Nothing so simple should be this good.

My God, it was so good I don't think I even inhaled.

I just swallowed and hoped there was enough left over tomorrow morning's sneak.

On Having Everything

My main problem is

...I have no problems

I was blessed with everything a woman

(and a man)

Could want.

I have money, a beautiful French name,

A body--tits and ass, you know, the works

An open mind, talent, a seductive voice

Deep piercing eyes that would bring any normal man to his knees,

Gorgeous hair, smooth skin, thick sensual lips, a radiant smile

And a striking appearance.

I'm never at a shortage of men

Probably never will be

I always get what I want

And occasionally they do too.

I only want the best

Because I'm worth it

I only give the best

Because if it comes from me you must be worth it.

Men tell me I'm sexy. I think so.

Men tell me they love me. That's nice.

I don't love

It causes too many problems

And I don't have any problems

I loved once

He was young, strong

And just as pretty a me

We looked good together--damn good

We met by accident

It was raining

I was speeding

He pulled me over

He asked for my license and had me verify the numbers

P362439

We fucked the night we met and the morning after

He made me feel good--real good--both times

And that was rare

We talked of problems, dreams, fantasies...

He had a lot of problems

I helped when I could

He told me my presence was enough.

We were careful

I took my pretty pastels everyday to avoid anymore unwanted problems

And one night he said, "I love you"

I said, "ok"

But he knew better...I thought

730 days passed for me to become as attached as he was

It happened one morning

It was raining

I woke up feeling sexy and wanted to share it

I rolled over and kissed his lips

He was still

I kissed again

He was still

I rolled him over

He was unconscious with this sorry excuse for a note pinned to his T-shirt

We slept nude

And when I realized he had no pulse

I did what anybody would do

I yelled, I screamed, I broke things, I damned him for leaving me this way

I was really hurt

Nobody's ever hurt me

I was stuck now

I had stopped taking my pretty pastels to surprise him that I had conceived

Shit, talk about a cramped style

60 years passed as I sat on the toilet unwinding that hanger

And I just wanted to shove it all the way up through my brains

So we could both rest in peace

WHAT WAS I SUPPOED TO DO? What was I supposed to do?

This was my gift to him and I had to take it back

I normally don't explain myself to people because I don't have to

But when I give myself to someone

I give all of me not just selections

Granted it may take some time but I gave him all of me

Because

I loved him...

And he never heard me say it

But that shouldn't have pushed him over the damn edge

He was weak and selfish and should have realized that all people show love differently

What was his damn problem?

Did I not give him enough?

I gave him everything I had which was everything!

Yes! I have everything! I got it all! If he wanted it I had it!

And he tried to take that away from me

Who in the hell did he think he was?

Nobody takes from me.

I'm a year older and wiser now

I'm still striking physically

Men still think I'm sexy--right?

My eyes still pierce

My voice is still seductive--please?

And my hair is down to my ass

I don't love

It causes too many problems

And I don't have any problems

I gained 60 years and lost 2 lives in 1 day

Ain't reality about a bitch?

But I learned how not to love

And I loved you...

...you selfish bastard.

Home at 32,000 Feet

The lights that greet me from below

Those lights that tell me "You are home"

Bring back so many memories

Smiles and joy

Yet draw tears

As childhood passes before my eyes

I have come to realize

These special lights from up above

Bring me peace

And radiate love

New York City at age 19

911

I had no idea. I was on my way to the gym and called to let my trainer know that I was going to be about 15 minutes late for our session. He told me not to worry about training because the gym is in turmoil over the chaos in New York.

"What happened?" I asked cautiously.

"Two planes just crashed into the World Trade Center. Aren't you watching the news honey?"

Being the former award-winning news anchor that I am, I really felt out of the loop. I hadn't been watching anything. I dropped off my daughters at school at 8:05, came home, and snoozed off for a while before heading to the gym. So I turned the TV on and what I saw left me numb. That morning I knew that the American quality of life as I knew it had shifted within my 45-minute nap.

The first thing I thought about was my Aunt Millie who works on Wall Street. That woman is my Angel on earth. She is 71 years old and looks not a day over 50. She is beautiful with flawless brown skin, sensitive brown eyes, a killer smile with straight white teeth, and natural hair that she has kept pulled back since I can remember. I grabbed my phone and called my Daddy. He assured me that Auntie is far enough from the wreckage and did his best to keep me calm. I don't know how well that worked, but he tried. It probably didn't help that I stayed glued to the television, but I finally got the strength to shut the damn thing off and go to the grocery store.

When I parked people I didn't even know greeted me. That shocked me. Normally grocery stores are full of… well…jack-asses who couldn't care less if they are in your way, run over your foot with a cart, or whatever, but shoppers had a new attitude that I hadn't seen probably since the Oklahoma City bombing. There were smiles, people helping one another, a lady who reminded me "He's got the whole world in His hands," and a great deal of eye contact. Men in their pickup trucks who usually display the confederate flag have now replaced it with "Old Glory" and blow their horns and wave at everyone in support. I am mortified at the massive loss of life and the coward's disregard for humanity, but I am relieved that Americans where I live are recognizing each other and the significance of living in this country.

I know I'm not the first to notice that people in this country are divisive. We still segregate ourselves along racial lines, religion, political party lines, language, national origin, and anything else we can find. As a black female (supposedly strikes one and two against me) I must admit that there have been times when I too have engaged in the same kinds of prejudiced and apathetic behavior that I now criticize vehemently. I know this country has issues. We know this country is hated, but if we continue to revel in hating each other then we should prepare for additional tragedies such as this because it is obvious that our REAL enemies know how and when to catch this country with its pants down.

The more I think about it the more grateful I am that I was asleep at the time of the suicide/murder missions. I really could not have handled witnessing live the second American Airliner plow into that second tower. I can barely handle listening to the testimonies of those who survived and those who are walking the streets looking for their loved ones. Watching Bryant Gumbel break down was enough to tear me up. He's one of the strongest and one of my most admired journalists. To watch him go against the grain of what is always preached about news reporters showing no emotion and remaining objective all went to hell. I really admired him for that. I'm sure there are many others who took the same route of subjective journalism.

When I was an anchor/reporter in Denver, my children watched as I cried and reported the news on tragedies like the Oklahoma City Bombing and the Jonbenet Ramsey murder. I was proud that my children at age three knew who Timothy McVeigh was and why he was sentenced to death, but at the same time it sickened me to have to explain such atrocities to toddlers.

My girls are eight now and I continued to cry the evening of 9/11 when my Kyetra was distraught with worry regarding her Aunt Millie whom I still had not heard from. Katana cried but stayed cool. She's always been like that. She internalizes a lot of stuff so I tend to watch her a bit closer. Kyetra is like her mother. She wears her emotions on her sleeve and all I could do was depend on God to give me the strength and wisdom to explain to my daughters why these bastards did what they did to our country. Bless their hearts, but my daughters still did not understand. They knew what went down, but their innocent hearts and tender spirits were not able to comprehend the type of hatred that these terrorists felt against the American people.

I see God everywhere now. "God bless the USA," "God help us," God is all over our nation now. I find that refreshing but think it is disgusting that it took such a tragedy for this nation to put God first. I'll tell you what, there is no separation of church and state today and prayer in schools is not a crime right now. Faith is all we have to depend on at this time and we as Americans only have each other. There is nothing left for us to do but love one another. We have no time for anything else.

This all-American love must include ALL Americans. Don't forget we do have Arab, Pakistani, Iraqi, and many other nationalities of AMERICAN people. This is not the time to trip on them! They are not our enemies. I am already reading several acts of senseless violence against these Americans, their businesses, and their homes. They are bleeding just as we are.

I thank God for my blessings to be alive this day and to share my feelings. I thank God for my health and the health of my family and loved ones near and far. I thank God that all of my family members and friends are accounted for after this day of devastation. I ask God to place his healing hands on the victims and their survivors. I ask God to bless ten fold all of the fire fighters, EMT squads, and volunteers who gave more of themselves than they knew they had. I thank God for America because despite all of our arguments, complaints, internal struggles, and daily conflicts I am grateful to live in the United States of America.

My prayer for this country is that this new spirit of patriotism, our faith in God, and our love for our fellow Americans continue from this day forward. I pray that it will not take another atrocity or massive loss of human lives for us to live as one nation under God indivisible with liberty and justice for all.

God...please bless America.

Y.W
9/14/01

Yvette Williams

Through the tropical green haze of your eyes I see you

Longing for him

Pride beams through your essence as you assume his role.

Labor is no stranger —no enemy

To provide is a blessing- responsibility runs deep

The measures we take depend on the circumstances we are dealt

And so you deal

Five endless days in fields of sweetness- there are no complaints

Only gratitude for the means

And the longing for his shadow

120 hours has elapsed- it is time

A mountain of bricks- your post awaits

Waiting for that sunset glimpse of the patriarchal shadow of life

Hours seem like minutes- minutes seem like hours

Until

His shadow is in view, his form is present, his being is clear

The mountain is no obstacle

And you run once again into the noble, loving, arms of security.

Thank you for sharing this part of your childhood with me.
I only hope I did your father justice with my words.

Life Sentence

It was Gallileo who said
"He who doesn't know the truth is a fool.
He who knows the truth and call it a lie...is a criminal."

Does that make me wrong if I know the truth
but don't tell you?

How about if I know the truth
but am afraid of it?

Would my fear of pain and rejection
really make me a criminal?

If my fears caused me to be viewed as a criminal
would you forgive me?

If I stole your heart
would that be considered felonious,
aggravated
misdemeanor

If this is a crime...
give me 25 to life
with you.

For A Brotha

Are you the man of my dreams
Or am I still just dreaming

I'll be your legs when yours are tired
I'll be your eyes when you can't see
I'll take your pain so you won't hurt

I'll be your spine-the foundation of your very existence
The backbone to your humanity
I'll be your strength, your grace, your image

I possess love that weak men can't handle

I exude passion that can break a man
How strong is your back

Every human is born with the ability to love
So few are willing to use it
Will you

A nation can rise no higher than its woman
I, woman, am descendant of you, man
Your rib that created me is my spine

Do you understand
We are one
So if a vertebrae slips
Our backbone becomes frail
And if our backbone becomes frail
Our foundation is weak
And if the foundation is weak
The structure collapses

Are you my King
    who completes my kingdom who will deserve me who will
    answer

Are you the man of my dreams
Or am I still just dreaming?

For my King

Talk to me
Reach for me
Know that I hear you
And won't let you fall

Trust in me
Lean on me
Believe that if you need strength
I will come through for you

Talk to me
If I can't be your friend
I can never be your lover

Reach for me
Hold on to my spirit
Don't let go

Trust in me
I exude the power that can strengthen any man
But you must put your trust in me
So I can pull you up

Up from oppression
Up from depression
Up from disgrace and disgust
Deceit and defeat

Hold on to me my brother
Grab tight -don't slip
I can't afford to lose you again
So I'll tighten my grip

Open up those big beautiful baby browns
And look
Look where you are
Look where you've come from
Look at me

I've cried for you
I've lied for you
I've lived for you
I've died for you

I can't survive without you
I am descendant of you
I am made of you
When you hurt- I hurt
When you bleed-I bleed

My beautiful Black man
If I can't run to you
Who can I run to
Where can I go
Who else will love me
the way I deserve to be loved
Make no mistake
There is no love like yours

I need you
I need your hands to touch me
I need you strength to lift me
I need your backbone to support me
I need your wisdom to teach me
I need your intuition to guide me
I need your arms to protect me

Do you respect me?

Do you realize my love for you goes deeper than
my sexuality
and
my sensuality
My love for you my brother is quality

I want to see you prosper
Like the King you once were
This is your domain
You do not realize your power
I have remained here to show you

Take what's rightfully yours
Take me
And
Take control

Spousal Support

loving you

is like

open heart surgery

performed with a pick-ax.

Scar Tissue

One thousand, one hundred twenty-two days of heaven
Destroyed by one night of hell
Twenty-six thousand, nine hundred twenty-eight hours of beauty
Depreciated within moments by a beast
One million, six hundred fifteen thousand, six hundred eighty
minutes of love
Shattered by your premeditated, self gratifying ejaculation

I feel so cheap
As if my love was merely sex
I feel as if my vagina now wears a clearance sticker
I see this relationship was like a 36 month long pap exam
--nothing more than a simple examination to search for something
that probably wasn't even there anyway

Father Time please heal me
Heal this internal scarring
Please rid the throbbing, painful reminders
Kill everlasting memories that I was once again something to do...
...instead of someone to love

Mother Nature, take my heart
I can handle no more pain...or at least prescribe an anesthetic
Maybe an anabolic steroid to harden my heart as well as my body
Shit, what's the point in looking like a lady if I'm never treated like
one?

I feel raped. Again!
Violated, stripped, and left for dead

The lies, deception, deceit, pain, abuse, apologies, reconciliation,
misplaced ejaculations, genuine and malicious orgasms, dishonesty,

attacks on my heart and mind and body and soul and womb and
very essence of being
Have once again been put on display
to laugh at

My screams of excruciating pain
as usual have gone unnoticed

But

Let it be known...

There is only so much pain that can be tolerated
before it and the joke are reciprocated.

Yvette Williams

3/12/01

I was ready to go that day

I had my car warmed up

A closed garage door, a bottle of feel nothing

And a hopeless attitude

I was ready to rock

My note was sent to all

But one

She pissed me off the night before

I was so ready to go

Lifeless

Loveless

Nothing left

It was so cold
Dark and full of hopelessness
-mine included

I hated it. Wanted to leave
-needed to stay

It was very cold
Full of panic and death
-mine included

It was hard to be there
I swallowed a lot of pride
-and sedatives

but that was all.

Yvette Williams

She could only grumble

She had no words

But a great smile

It had eaten at her

A 90-year old looking infant

Not yet 70

She couldn't eat, wash, or relieve herself

She lost it all

Except her heart

She loved to fix my blankets

I had so many

It was deathly cold in there

Frightened by a 3:00am shadow

My blankets were messed up

I left eleven hours later

But not without returning the favor.

your dishonesty...

is a sharp pain that starts between my legs,

cuts through my guts,

twists around my heart,

punctures both my lungs,

travels up my esophagus,

circles within my mouth,

and assists my lips and tongue to form the words...

...fuck you.

you are a bitch.

you are the epitome of
a bitch.

you are the raw, cynical, uncut, fucked up spirit of
a bitch

you are the ruthless, heinous, warped, demented asshole once
suspected of being
a bitch

you are the spineless, weak, yellow-bellied soul of
a bitch

now…

Bark nigga.

I used to call him "dark and lovely" now I just call him dark

He said, "I think braids are a style for lazy black women."

"Oh." I replied and kept mine in.

Regarding the white girl six months later he said, "She meant nothing to me, I didn't mean to hurt you. I felt insecure and threatened. I'm sorry. I'm really sorry."

"Yes. You really are." I replied.

and the beat goes on…

Reality Check

I won't do it

I won't scream yell and cry

I won't act like a weak bitch

You've already done that

I won't cut your throat

Even though you've cut mine

I won't screw your friend

There is no challenge -he wants me

I won't strike your face

As much as I lust over it

I won't act a fool

I won't break your neck

I won't screw your friend

I won't bomb your house

I won't hurt myself

I won't

I can't

stop loving you

Yvette Williams

For My King
(part 2)

When I close my eyes

I see your mistake

When I lick my lips

I taste your lies

Every step I take

I feel your so-called love

it's a constant 1-2 punch in the crotch

that spreads through my guts and attacks my backbone

(by the way what happened to yours?)

This pain has curved my spine, imploded my lungs

and severed my heart

(much like the way you severed my trust)

You were my King

The man of my dreams

I only thank you

...for waking me up.

The Punch line

I miss what we had

~~I miss what we had~~

I miss what I *thought* we had

I don't even know what we were.

You were supposed to be the one

The one who was different

The one who loved me unconditionally not just until the work of maintaining

became challenging

I didn't pick you, you picked me

You loved me for my strength, now you left me over it.

The blessing and the curse huh?

And you wonder what makes me so tough

It's dealing with bullshit like yours that adds fuel to the fire and another layer of armor

The traits that you said drew you to me

are now the traits you can't handle.

What do you want a weak bitch? Submission? I thought that was what you didn't want.

You said you wanted a challenge, you got one, and you punked out.

…just like the rest.

I have already forgiven you, but I will never forget.

Rebound Man

Just shut up and take off your clothes
I only have an hour before I have to go
He's supposed to call me
I can't miss that call
He'll know

Forty-five minutes left
I'm giving away everything that was once his
I feel so powerful
Maybe this is how he felt
I want every thrust to stab his heart like pins in a voodoo doll

That was cool

I may come back
Power runs down my legs
My heart is in synch with some one else
The third may have stopped by now
Thank you gorgeous. I'm out of time.
I need to clean up and catch his call

Hmm, you truly are the best friend he has.

Ode to a jack-ass

I wanted to mail you a dead rat

But with the anthrax scares going on at the time

It was not in my best interest

So I fantasized about you

About breaking your neck

About piercing your skin

Layer by layer

And viewing your blood

As it turns from blue to red when it comes in contact with the air

I smiled as I dislocated your joints

One by one

And as I went to sever your spine

I realized

…you never had one.

Reconcile

As he lays
There's a certain air of innocence about him
Makes me wonder how something this sweet could dance with the
devil

As he lays
My heart fills with emotion
My eyes with tears
My mind with wonder

As he lays
He radiates an energy of hope that eases my soul to once again
conform to his as one

As he lays
Every breath he takes-a sigh of relief
Every toss and turn-tension released
My eyes behold such beauty
Dare I love him again?

As he lays
My body draws hesitantly
I smell his skin
We touch
He's hot
It's just like old times
but I pray even better

Last Chance

I carried your burdens-you broke my back

I supported your causes-you ignored me

I loved you faithfully-you sold me out

I dried your tears-you slapped my face

I embraced your being-you disgraced my name

But I accepted you over and over and over

And I hate it

I swear,

I will always love you Black man

But please don't give me another reason to dislike you.

Senon -in simile

like getting the honey just right in your tea

like the lip color that runs flawless across your lips

like a chilled German Riesling with a mild effervescence

like singing that once in a lifetime note and capturing it on recording

like reaching point B and never catching a red light

like your smile when you don't know I'm staring

like your arms when you think it may not matter

like your eyes when I view your soul

like your laugh when its depth reaches my heart

like your spirit -visible to the touch, tender to the eye, fragrant to the soul

simplicity was never so perfect

By right he should be the one of the most insensitive, cold-hearted people ever. Instead he is lost. Trapped in a matrix if you will. Caught between the heaven he could easily obtain and the hell he has lived in and refers to as his "comfort zone."

When I met him he had scars. The visible scars were forgiven. The hidden scars were problematic. Cigarette burns, broken bones, darts- (I guess someone felt the need to use this baby's face as target practice for some sort of tournament) I thought these things happened to people on television. Even at thirty-four years of age these scars obviously never healed physically or psychologically.

Those who view him aesthetically will never know him. The same eyes that cried at birth were the same eyes that welled up refusing to release the venom he called tears. I suppose when you've screamed in pain for the first several years of your life, you view tears as some sort of weakness. In a certain light his brown eyes looked black and cold, but the deeper I looked the browner they became. I began to really learn the thirty-four year old man who still waited to be held, loved, and comforted, yet refused to reciprocate.

The game was easy initially. We had good times. The proposal was a surprise, the answer was yes, the ceremony was beautiful, and the chaos began.

I saw sides of him that were insane. He could laugh one minute and be ready to kill the next. I knew there was a term for this but I wasn't sure what it was. I'm a communicator. He was the antithesis. I talk and when my other half shut down on me my mind went dangerously erratic. All of my worst fears came into play and the baggage from past relationships crashed at 80 miles an hour onto the conveyer belt of my psyche. I just knew he was running behind my back, which in my mind is the worst possible act of disrespect.

He always spoke on how he responds to disrespect, but if this were true then why wasn't he kicking his own ass? Days would pass and not a word from him. His brown eyes turned black again and my reserve bank of inner-strength was running low.

Through the arguments, accusations, and busted illusions I was afraid to admit that I had made a terrible mistake by getting married. I loved him and I thought he loved me, but I was done fighting with the three or more personalities that cohabitated within this walking corpse. The eyes I fell in love with were screaming for something, and the more I tried to help the more distant he became. That was agonizing. I was the one who reached out to alleviate pain and suffering. It was me. I was there. When he believed in his heart that no one gave a damn and no one understood, I did. When he was pissed, I was pissed. When he was happy, I was happy. When he called, I responded. I was never too proud to be his wife even when he and other folks told me that I deserved better or that he wasn't worthy of me. The pain came in accepting that they were right. I couldn't take it anymore. One good day, three bad days; one good week, two bad weeks, what the hell was going on?

I accept that I never read his eyes properly in the beginning. Others saw what I chose not to see. I saw him recently and his eyes are still dark, his short hair is a tangled mess, and he looks as if he had given up on life. He looks as if he rarely smiles, and his caramel colored skin is as pale as a dying summer flower. It is clear to me that he is reaping what he sowed and that life has brought him to his knees. I hope he figures out soon that he is in the perfect position to pray.

Yvette Williams

Marriage in springtime

The smell of fertilizer carelessly blowing my way -damn near choking me to death- was indicative of the kind of day it was going to be. I was walking up Perry Street on my way to the courthouse. I'd been struggling with my marriage for months, which is pretty sad since I had only been married for a year and a couple of months.

I had asked him that day what was to come of this "holy matrimony." He said he didn't know. Another lie. He didn't care. We separated two months after our first anniversary. I'm surprised we even made it that far since he emotionally (and sexually) left the marriage three months after our wedding. "Trial and error" he called it. It makes me wonder why the simple bastard proposed in the first place.

Was he Linus and I the blanket which he dragged around carelessly while sucking his thumb claiming to be something and someone he wasn't? Why was it that three months into our marriage he was laid up with a ninety pound, cocaine addicted, alcoholic, high school dropout? Why wasn't I given the opportunity in wedlock that others had on the outside?

"Linus" obviously saw security in me. I'm a sista with a lot to offer. Aside from my love which is immeasurable, I'm a 13-year veteran of broadcasting (of which I am still reaping the benefits), I enjoy a fulfilling career as an educator and professional vocalist, I'm physically fit, and after crossing 40 I still turn a few heads so I can't look that bad. Some would say I have it going on and I have learned that my success was the problem.

I used to blame myself for this disaster but now I realize and accept that I did my best. What pisses me off the most is the time and money I wasted with this cat. Yes, I mentioned money because there was a great deal of it that was pretty much burned in effigy if you know what I mean (travel, gowns, rings, and that was before the ceremony). Call me shallow if you wish, but had I known I would have to spend thousands of dollars afterward to baby-sit what would be my husband, of course I would have never walked down the aisle. Yet I have to admit I looked damn good in that dress.

People, the next time any man tells me that I "can do better" or he is "not worthy of my love" I'm going to assume he knows more than I do and run like hell. I would advise the same.

Looking back, they say hindsight is always 20/20, I admit to ignoring many red flags that were shaking their asses in my face. I also accept that I settled for less than what I deserve. I believed there was good in him and was ready to become the superhero who would capitalize on that and reap the rewards. The best reward I gave myself was getting out. Looking forward I concur that no one can help a person who refuses to help himself. To feel so inferior to a woman who loves you as you are (flaws and all), that one attempts to justify the worst possible act of betrayal in order to feel superior is an act which will always confuse me. He hand picked at the bottom of the barrel in an attempt to feel worthy when all he had to do was come home.

On that day as I inhaled the foul stench of spring, I realized it was comparable to my marriage. Pure…uncut…bullshit.

Success Is the Best Revenge

To all those who said it couldn't be done

This one's for you

To those who laughed

This one's for you

To all those who tried to interfere (and there have been many)

This one's for you

To my old 1213 college roommates who told me I don't sing as well as I thought

You're right. I sing even better

This one's for you

To the donor who said "They ain't mine"

This one's for you

To the same sorry simpleton who was outraged over my appointing a white man to be the legal Godfather of my children...

Get a grip, get a job, and get responsible. Until then...

Shut the fuck up!

This one's for you

For Pie and Tootie, everything I do I do for you. My desire is to be your role model.

My life's for you

To all single mothers, cheated hearts, and victims of circumstance

This one's for you

For Cree, I'm so glad you realized that love is not painful. I have missed you Sista

This one's for you

To the college bitches who always made time to dog me out over trivial bullshit

This one's for you

For Rita, the professor I'll never forget and the first writer who believed in me.

Thank you.

This one's for you

For Michael, you treated me like a queen while I was getting treated like a dog.

the mistake was mine, please forgive me

This one's for you

For my "Skillet" I will never have another like you. You are my friend, my family, and I love you for eternity. I'll never forget our wrestling matches the year we "cohabitated" in Harrison Hall the summer of 1989. HA! Who's laughing now? I think we are.

This one's for you

Yvette Williams

For the one and only Nino. What the hell can I say? You have been everything- a father, friend, guardian, confidant and to simply tell you that I love you would be insulting.

This one's for you

For the Duke- you hit me in the back of the head when it was down and kicked my feet when they dragged, always encouraged the music and always had time to listen to and understand your cussing, hard-headed daughter

This one's for you

For my Mommy who rushed to my side when I was ready to check out, and dealt with my rebellion. Thank you for sticking with me through the rough years.

This one's for you

To all those who are able to laugh--back

This one's for you

To those who always tried to adjust my attitude by attempting to tear it down

You've only added fuel to the fire

This one's for you

To all those who are able to smile while being screwed over and actually look sincere

This one's for you

For all my sisters who remain black, and blue and purple and dead all in the name of love

You are not forgotten

This one's for you

To our authoritative figures who still have problems effectively determining a rape charge

This one's for you

To the men in blue who are here to serve and protect

You are here to protect us but who protects us from you?

Keep your weapons loaded if you want to but behold the eyes upon you

This one's for you

To our know-it-all Republicans who reformed welfare without reforming the deadbeats who cause it in the first place

Check yourselves and the facts before you pass anymore feel good laws ok?

This one's for you

To all school officials public and private who still feel no need to include REAL African American, Native American, Latino/Hispanic or any other ethnic history in your curriculums. You say knowledge is power. Does that depend on what you are?

The history books you teach from are incomplete and inaccurate, and WE know it.

This one's for you

Did I make you uncomfortable?

Yvette Williams

Does the truth hurt?

No need to run anymore. I don't.

Stand up and face up.

I have.

I have been the victim, but there comes a point when that title becomes a choice.

I've been weak, the butt of all your jokes, called helpless, hopeless, and high-risk

I've been raped, robbed, violated, forgotten, deserted, insulted, attacked, beaten, hated, and hurt.

I have sighed, cried, wasted too much time, rebelled, yelled

And for what?

You have kept me down because I allowed you. I am at fault.

My self-esteem was destroyed, I lost my pride, my dignity, my self-respect

But I never lost my mind

With that I was able to retrieve motivation, drive, power and this "so what" attitude

So, now what?

They say success is the best revenge and I am laughing...

...my ass off.

Give My Regards To Restrooms

There is just something about using the restroom in the privacy of my own home that gives me a great deal of comfort. Actually, there are a plethora of issues that contribute to this sense of security.

I remember growing up listening to my father preach "the word" about sanitation and general hygiene. My Baba worked as a produce clerk at the local grocery stores and sanitation was something he held sacred. If we crossed the boundaries of proper cleanliness a severe tongue-lashing was just around the corner.

Aside of frequent lectures as a child, I think the main reason I find insecurity in public restrooms-especially at my places of employment-comes from witnessing the very things my father warned me about time after time. I can't begin to count the incidents in which I have seen people use the restroom, walk out of the stall, smile and greet me, and walk straight out the door. No anti-bacterial wash, no hand friction under some water, no nothing. Unsanitary acts such as that send my imagination into a hygienic frenzy. What do these people view as clean? How are they living at home? How can they use the restroom, not wash, and go about their business? From that point, all I can picture is these nasty individuals wiping their asses and preparing meals.

In all public restaurants there are signs that clearly read "Employees must wash hands before returning to work." Does that exempt the rest of the world from washing after wiping?

I have to admit I have been known to hold my water up to an incredible five hours a time because I don't want to subject myself to this filth. If I know what I'm going to see will sicken me then why go through it? My physician is the first to go off on me about my bladder busting habit. I love my doctor because she has no problem letting me know how badly I'm screwing up. She thinks

I have lost my mind at times, but she will generally see things my way and help survive at my own standards so I don't kill myself.

Using the restroom at work is a fate worse than death for me. At my current position I thank God my children get out of school at 2:30. Not only is a chance to see their bright smiling faces during the day and hear about all the hardships of being a seven-year old, but it also gives me a chance to "use it" and be secure.

I have to admit I'm the first to get an upset stomach at work when I have to meet clients, listeners and corporate figures. When they extend their hand, I just look at it. Of course working in the world of corporate and political correctness I am obligated to shake hands all the time, but you can best believe I am running to the sink or grabbing my bottle of anti-bac once it's over.

Hand washing has come full circle in my life because I'm constantly badgering my girls about the same things my father lectured me about. People's hands are nastier than their mouths. You hear all the time that more illnesses are contracted from shaking hands than kissing. I remember in my childhood days of rebellion (I stress childhood because I'm still in my rebellion phase) trying to go against my father and running out of the bathroom without washing my hands. I was so overridden with guilt and shame that I had no choice to give in and walk (with my tail between my legs) back up the stairs, grab that square goldenrod bar of Dial soap, and get down to business.

Public restrooms? It had better be a life-threatening emergency and with children by your side they happen frequently, but know that I step into that war zone prepared for battle. How people can live with themselves and their unsanitary habits is beyond me. My father was never able to answer my question of "Why?" And that experience has come full circle for me with my children. I love seeing the looks of horror and nausea on their faces as someone steps right out of a stall and out the doors.

"Mommy that woman didn't..."

"Shhh." I interrupt. "You just make sure *you* handle up on business."

I tell you what, I'll be squirming worming in my seat and doing the "pee-pee dance" before I subject my body and my health-regardless as to whether the stall has paper liners or not. What I see on a day-to-day basis is enough to make me keep my hands in my pockets, allow my bladder to explode, and join Michael Jackson in his hyperbolic chamber.

Don't Call Me Sista

Yeah sure we are all brothers and sisters in God's way, but when the first thing outta your mouth to me is "I'm not prejudiced! I date Black guys." Please don't get offended when I roll my eyes and give you the finger. I can certainly appreciate your attraction to my men. They are beautiful, but so much more than an object that you can use to rebel against your racist parents.

Please don't call me "Sista." That nauseates me. I'm sure you're a bit let down but let me explain. When you can carry the burdens of an entire people for 500 years, or remain the backbone of a man, yet still allow him to feel as if he is one, or accept the fact that you are not the socially accepted trend of what his idea of beauty should be, then you will get it.

Don't address me as "girl" either. I am not your girl. That word takes me back before my time to an era that you choose to forget. Try referring to a Black man as "boy" even in the heat of the moment and watch it all come to a screeching halt. Sleeping with a Black man is not the same as loving a Black man. Bonding with a Black man should not require being on your knees.

You are no better, sexier, smarter or more beautiful than any of my sisters or me and vice versa. But I need to hip you to some information that has given some of you false ammunition to roll with. Black men love Black women. I don't care if you're in the bed with one or not. They love us. The problem is that many Black men have been systematically conditioned since slavery to believe that you are better than I am. And since we are there...

You turned your heads when your husbands, fathers, and brothers raped and molested us in the night- sometimes straight out of your bed. You knew. Don't act shocked. You were not carrying your husband's baby. I was. If I chose not to, I was killed.

Point blank. You call me sista now, but where were you when I needed you as a woman back then?

The women's liberation movement was for you. No, sweetheart it was not for me. Black women were not allowed to be a part of your women's lib shit. You fought for the rights of Black men before you fought for my rights. I guess that was when your lust started kickin' in. The Women's Rights era was a time, which placed further division between you and I because you felt of course that you were the real "women" and of course you felt you were "right."

I can totally understand where your ego comes from. Your White male counterparts have placed you on pedestals for years. My people were beaten into submission to respect you. My men were warned never to touch or even look at you. Hmm, maybe somebody was threatened? You were viewed as innocent, pure, and sin-free. The history is written, read it. I'm not delivering anything new, and I damned sure did not create this race-sex hierarchy.

Don't get me wrong though. I'm not saying that there aren't Black men and White women who have mutual relationships full of love, respect, fidelity, and compassion. What I am getting at is the stupid-ass comments that you've tossed at me directly or indirectly, that imply that you are "one up" on me because you "have a Black man in your bed" and I don't, have now been kicked back at you.

Before you hate me, try to understand what's been put out there. You don't have to like me, or what I'm saying, but understand that there must be some sort of meeting of the minds or mouths that needs to occur. I don't hate you. I have never hated you. What I hate is our history. There is so much that needs to be mended before we can bond as women, and there is even more that will be rectified between us before I will ever allow you to refer to me as "sista."

Vanilla Latte

I salute you my Sistas
My Vanilla latte sistas
My milk chocolate Sistas
My mocha crème Sistas
My sandy brown, naturally-blond Sistas
My green, blue and gray eyed Sistas
My "light bright damn near white" Sistas
My Sistas who could "pass" but refuse
My Sistas who are scorned for not being "Black enuf"
My Sistas who tolerate "Exactly what race do you belong to" in the
    corporate workplace
My Sistas who are asked, "How do black women feel about you
    dating <u>their</u> men?"
My Sistas who go outta their way to prove they are

I hear your cries-
        From the plantation of the adulterous slave master
        forcing you into submission
        To the insecure CEO who grasps at any reason to
        DIScredit,
        DISgrace and DISmiss you since you're threatening with
        your talent, beauty
        and skillz
I despise your struggle
        Too black for one world
        Too white for another
I feel your pain
        When you hurt, I hurt
        When you are insulted
        We ALL are insulted
        Save your energy. You have nothing to prove.

I salute you my Sistas
My vanilla latte Sistas

Holding your heads high
As you live the worst of both worlds.

For Sarah (Sissy) & Lisa
2/20/2001

Yvette Williams

The families I met who suffered
I can't help but be resentful
Mommies without their babies-I bled for them
Others without limbs unconscious from the pain
Terrorist is too weak a word
Holding hands with those I saw on TV-their pain penetrated me
You did this

Mastermind of this massive loss of life
Collateral damage huh?
Victim after victim they testified
Everyday living in hell from your cowardice act
Intravenous jurisprudence
God says to forgive but I can't. How can they?
Hell's permanent resident. May your ass burn eternally.

Talking Black Jack

I consider myself to be a seasoned professional-at least I'd like to think so. I give a lot to my community and humanity. I give of my time, services, and finances. I proudly support my own, but I must admit when I go out into my community my heart keeps getting broken by my people who seem to think I'm not "Black enough" because of the way I speak.

There is nothing extraordinary about my speaking habits. I have no accent-except when I get really pissed off, then the New Yorker comes back alive. I have simply been informed that my problem is that I speak "white" or too proper. Except for in appropriate settings, I just don't get into the street slang that I'm expected to.

Why this is still an issue in the Obama era is beyond me, but I'd like to know if talking white means speaking properly then what the hell is talking black? I'll tell you what, I'm paying back thousands in federal student loans for my undergraduate, graduate, and doctoral degrees and I'll be damned if I am going to speak like Mushmouth. If this is what is expected of me as a professional African American woman who has the responsibility to represent others, then call me what you will.

Why am I still classified as "acting White" for speaking well and progressing? We as African American people have always suffered. We have also put ourselves through plenty of unnecessary suffering. Why are we still here?

And what I get from White folks is just as stupid. I will never forget a former radio Program Director telling me (on the job mind you) that I was the "Whitest Black girl he's ever met."

You will never understand the pain I feel when I speak to my people and they ask me why I speak the way I do. I've even had some of us laugh or try to mock me. African American women that

I have assisted in bettering themselves have accused me of thinking that I am better. Excuse me sista, if I thought I was better, I would offer nothing.

There are so many unanswered questions. Unfortunately, I can only assume that this treatment comes from living in a society that glorifies and sensationalizes negativity and having less.

As sick as it sounds positivity doesn't make headlines. I've noticed in my years of working in news that so many people don't give a damn about the stories that leave a positive mark on communities. We want the dirt, the juice, the death and destruction, the convictions, incarcerations, and executions. No one gives a damn about the well-spoken African American professionals in the communities who bend over backward trying to make the slightest difference. It's bad enough when you see a brother or sista on the television they're either in handcuffs, they're fighting, or showing their ass on reality TV. Yet, when we are finally able to get a glimpse of one making strides they are labeled bourgeois, stuck-up, and White and it's unfortunate as hell.

Holla.

Tired and tuckered out

I remember that bloody summer in Denver.

Shots rang through the night so frequently that they formed a
rhythm and became natural

Shattered glass formed my make shift cymbal as the sounds of
running feet became my snare

It was hot

I would rub on them to verify movement.
Alive and kicking inside of me

My bed wasn't the best
Drove a stick so I could never quite get in a comfortable position as
the three of us rested
outside of your apartment
Seven months- so the heat was intensified if that was even possible.

I knocked since you "borrowed" my key

No answer as the party ensued

It was late. You had company.
Remember?

A tap at my room window
They peeped in my car from time to time wondering why
And who did this

"Miss Sophisticated" one of them called me after he asked me if I
needed anything.

Anything…is what they offered.
I smiled at one in particular.
The sincerity in his eyes penetrated the dark rag that covered his face.
I said no thank you because karma is a bitch.
He must have been a daddy
He was disturbed as he walked away slowly from my room on wheels

They protected me that night

Made me wonder who the real criminals were

I'm still the same woman from that event twenty years ago
The only real differences are the Dr. that will precede my name and grown twins

The work is done, that chapter has ended

Now, I have company
And the door is closed.

Danny

I missed you so dearly today

I'm not sure why

Today was different

I was dazed by thoughts of you

I saw your face everywhere

I felt your spirit rest on my shoulder

(much like the way you rest your head)

There was an energy that moved me today

Perhaps originating from anticipation of seeing you smile at me

I missed you madly today

it was a longing for what makes me happy

Being with you gives me an escape from reality

(because I still feel like you're a dream)

And if this is true

...may I never awaken

Piece of Mind

When I told myself I was finally going to sit down and write about my relationships I first thought to myself, "Where the hell do I start?" Being where I am now as compared to where I have been such a short time ago makes me feel as if I have no beginning in which to share. I have only a shady, confusing, one-sided, massive pile of shit in the middle of my life, which I am still trying to sort through.

First, let me state for the record that I love men. I am not a male basher, and I am one of the few women who still idealize the old fashioned, stone aged mentality that men are to provide and protect. Well, as a single mother of twins who's "baby-daddy" told me that I'm nothing more than a sorry-ass welfare mother who'd never amount to shit, I'd say I'm still not in my right mind for having these beliefs. I must admit at times I dwelled in the "men ain't shit mentality." I wouldn't be female if I didn't. But I have recently adopted a new practice called self-preservation.

I have been told countless times (especially by my father) that I have crappy taste in men. Not as far as looks are concerned but regarding the actual person I choose to give myself to. They've been womanizing, insecure punks who wallow in the systematic brainwashing of Black men. I have chosen nothing but losers and after all of the self-realization courses taken during my graduate studies, I can accept fault for dealing with and selecting these individuals who really had no legitimate place in my life.

Typically, I am a private person. I tell you only what I feel you need to know. However, in this case I actually feel that "putting it all out there" may help another sista in need and I wish I would have had the same support back when I was screwing up.

My first screw up was that I always put my man before myself. No man ever came before my children, just before me. I guess

---

I basically ignored what I was doing and justified my actions by trusting men who said that they "love God and put the Lord first" in their lives. Lightening should have struck when those lies were told.

I have often been told (and for a while never believed) that some people are put in our lives not for a lifetime but for a lesson. If ever I learned a lesson with the last jackass it was how, when, and why to set boundaries.

As women we typically put ourselves last in all we do and I was no exception. I was extremely foolish and I am still learning. The next man I love, I will love with sense. I will not lose who I am in this person. I will not stop living my life the way I live it in order to keep up with this man. We will enhance each other, which is something I have never experienced before. However, I will go on without him if the relationship becomes unhealthy.

I learned how to love better by taking care of myself. In short, I learned to set boundaries and stick to them in order to survive. Most of us don't do this, and I know this is why my relationships did not last. I learned that I am someone with feelings and needs and if those needs are not met and cannot be met, then it is clearly time to move on. Years later, I can still feel how unhealthy my marriage and past relationships were. I still get the nausea and clenched fists. Back then my mind was stuck in the set of "It has already been so long. Why quit now? I don't want to start over and I can fix it." I understand now that no, I can't fix what ain't meant to be. I am not this dude's maintenance problem. I am not superwoman. I do not wear a cape and I am not going to change the force. It's gon' be what it's gon be. At that time I thought I was invincible when in actuality I was invisible to him as well as myself. He didn't hear me crying because I didn't hear me crying. He didn't give a damn about me because I didn't give a damn about me.

I simply thank God for opening my eyes enough to see that love is not blind, painful, stupid, or worthless. I also had to take into account that if good, healthy relationships were easy, everybody would have one. I see that I bring mad baggage to the table (I am working on this) and many men carry a Samsonite chock full of their own stuff. Men have quirks that can be irritating and I am still very selfish and plan to remain that way until I accomplish the goals that I wasn't able to reach due to my role as babysitter disguised as a wife. I finally get that I am only me and I am still working to get that right.

One of my single homegirls who used to swear that I had it going on, once asked me how I manage to keep it together with these brothers. I told her the truth. I don't. All I can do is me. I hated to bust her bubble and inform her that I am just as fragile as she is, but even though the truth hurts most of the time, once the lesson has been learned it will always set you free.

I know I'm not a counselor even though I've paid my weight in sessions to be called one, but my sistas, it is hard to love us. Not because we are too difficult, but because we are too damn deep. Our strength overwhelms even ourselves. That is what makes us so beautiful. When a sista loves you, we really love you. We love with our whole selves. There is no breakdown. There are no boundaries and that is where we must draw a small line in the sand before another simple undertow washes away yet another castle.

Dearest Whitney,

As the world says goodbye to you, I share that I'm still stricken with pain. I understand your pain, strife, and demons. I know your struggle to want to be the best and I overstand your struggle to simply exist. Your path was simply that-your path. Only you knew your pain and I fully understand the heartbreak of needing help and not wanting to or even knowing how to ask. I understand giving your heart to those who NEVER deserved it and still feel the pain from that rejection and abuse. I grieve for your human side more than the performer. I will always love and respect you. Your voice will never be replaced. They can shatter glass and scream as loud and high as they like. No voice will touch the richness and clarity as the gift you gave us. You will always be "the voice." Be with God now, please kiss Michael for me, and please rest in peace. –Yvette 2/18/12

Tengo solo unas pocas palabras para agradecerte
Por validar mi tono
Por autenticar mi profundidad
Por legalizar mi bajo

I have few words to thank you
For validating my tone
For authenticating my depth
For legalizing my bass

Por muchos años tuve miedo que mi voz fuera demasiado para
oídos corrientes,
hasta que estudié la tuya

For years I feared my voice was too much for mainstream ears
Until I studied yours

Le diste significado a contralto
Pusiste poder detrás de proyección
Me permitiste apreciar la riqueza que mi voz ha adquirido

You gave meaning to contralto
Put power behind projection
Allowed me to appreciate the richness my voice has acquired

Ahora, por medio de la tuya
Me encanta mi tono
Valoro mi profundidad
Mi bajo es chévere
Soy como tú, la gran contralto

Now through yours
I love my tone
I treasure my depth
I dig my bass
I am, like you, the true contralto

Te doy las gracias y te extraño.

I thank you and I miss you.

AZUCAR!

Para Celia- descansa en paz

Yvette Williams

To a hawk

how i envy you
the way you glide

not a care

you move-so still
undetected
beautiful
black stealth

how i envy your gift
of grace
your ability to be
one's worst nightmare
and another's dream

black predator
how i wish

Another challenging day

Just because I smile doesn't mean everything is good.
It means I choose to find happiness amongst the challenges.

Just because I dance doesn't mean I'm not in pain.
It means I choose rehabilitation that I love.

Just because I present well, doesn't mean I'm wealthy.
It means I choose to exhibit fabulous regardless.

I am not always what you think.

Perception is not always reality.

I simply choose to live.

A long overdue thank you note

Dear Tom,

I need to share with you how grateful I am that you entered into my life seventeen years ago.

While others were writing me off as a single mother with a set of toddler twins, you saw talent that you took on to develop into awards, prestige, and respect.

You never downgraded me as a person -even though you killed my news scripts and edited one so badly that I barely had anything to say when the news sounder went off and my mike became hot. I can laugh...now.

You taught me to be strong as hell and at times that backfires on me, but I'd rather be too strong than too weak any day. You put a fire under me that continues to grow and draws others to me who seek that same support, truth, and, compassion that you have given me.

You taught me to challenge authority (hell you taught me to challenge everything), to never accept "No" or "I don't know" as answers where they are not warranted, and you taught me how to make my own way through yours.

I am successful. I am happy, and I am so grateful that you believed in me.

Much love,
Troubleshooter Diva

When I looked into your eyes
Through all the misunderstandings, normal teenage issues, and rebellion,
I saw myself.

A girl trying to discover her purpose
A girl trying to understand what her contributions to society and the world would be
A girl in the process of becoming

Through your tears
I saw hope, dreams, and a desire to succeed
And that same underlying grin that says " Brace yourselves, I'm about to kick ass and take names."

Through my tears
I pray that you saw unconditional love, encouragement, and strength should you feel weak. Pride is a gross understatement.
My words are not what I want them to be for you. I can't focus.

My heart feels punctured.
My soul feels imbalanced.
My home feels awkward.

We thought this would be so easy.

I've never claimed to have the strength that others see in me.
Honestly, I don't understand it.
Only wanted to do my best with you- whatever that took.
I admitted to making plenty of mistakes- and will make more.
This pain is temporary- I understand that.

And maybe I did spoil you, and give you too much, and tolerate what I shouldn't have,
But if last night was the end result...

Then we did the damn thang.

That night when you said that you had nothing left here, it hit me.
And I believed you
You have truly outgrown this place
The four walls I provided no longer shelter you
They now hinder you

That night when you said you had nothing left here, it hit me.
You now have all of the tools you need to positively impact society
You are a star waiting to shine even brighter
You have a stage greater than your last to conquer

Two weeks we sat in this house staring at each other
Wondering what to do
Wondering what to say
Wondering what she was doing
Wondering if she was thinking about us as much as we were her

We sat together and counted down

I prayed returning home without the second
Would be easier than the first
It wasn't
I was destroyed entering an empty home

I had tears in my eyes that night but I cried even harder
When you said
You have nothing left here
Except me.

I love you Pie, Pum 9/2011

Yvette Williams

9 / 11 / 11

As a writer and a native New Yorker I figured I would have some profound words on this tenth anniversary of 9/11.

Yet I have no words.

I only have images that still haunt me, voices that still speak to me, and her spirit
which still comforts me and strokes my hair until I fall asleep.

Still I can produce no words that I deem effective enough on this day.

I was sick with fear.

She made it home but her body deteriorated month by month.

I blame that day.

I blame those cowards.

She'd still be here I believe. She was so full of joy and grace.

I do my best to forgive as God demands, but I'd be a liar if I said that I was good at it.

R.I.P. my lady. –Your loving niece

Commencement

My Tio (Uncle Butch) recently told me that I don't accept compliments well so to him right now I proudly say "Thank you Tio." I graciously thank all others who have complimented me on a job well done. I take pride in my accomplishments, but none have been more rewarding than watching my twin daughters walk across the stage receiving their high school diplomas and head on their way to college with scholarships. The pride I feel is overwhelming and I feel so blessed and accomplished as a single mother to raise such successful young ladies.

However, people just do not realize what I have endured. To ask me such a stupid question as "What are you going to do after the twins graduate?" Really? I laugh to that.

What am I expected to do? Roll over and die? Get knocked up AGAIN and start over? That question is just as stupid as the ones I got when I had them. "What are you going to do with twins?" "How are your going to raise both of them?" How about these: "Which one is your favorite?" "What do you do when they both cry?" I remember telling that twit "I just pick my favorite and keep it moving. Duh!"

I plan to live my life. I plan to continue to love and enjoy my daughters as adults. I plan to work on a relationship with a man who is truly worthy of me. I plan to release this book (smile). I plan to record more music. I plan to sing. I plan to rest well and enjoy the end of the daily rat race. I plan to travel. I plan to live my life with an unhurried sense of time. I plan to be addressed at Dr. Yvette "Diva" Williams. I plan to adopt a few animals. I plan to enjoy the new lives and future careers of my daughters. I plan to be in attendance for all of their future accomplishments and families. This is by no means the end. This is the beginning.

While my heart beams with pride over my two beautiful and

talented daughters, I must say that this journey was not easy. The sacrifices were deep and went beyond finances. There were days when I thought I was going to lose my life due to the stress. I have NEVER had one job. I wouldn't know what one job felt like. Child support was a fucking joke. The Colorado court system was always so backed up that I could never get a fair shake at what was owed to these children, and the damn deadbeat was on the run for years. The arrearages would pay for a full year of private college alone, but I suppose the damage is done now and he is the only one missing out right? I wonder.

I do not regret a day with my daughters, but I will admit that raising twins alone kicked my ass! My life has been non-stop hustle and flow and ladies please listen when I say that this is not a job that should be done alone. It breaks my heart when I hear ladies say that they will "give a man a baby." Children are not gifts. They are humans. They are commitments for life. They require sacrifices and daily self-reality checks. Raising children takes teamwork, and nothing sucked more than being mommy and daddy to my kids when I was blessed with having both of my parents. I didn't know how to explain that. While I appreciated being honored on Father's Day, that shit just wasn't acceptable to me.

Ladies, if your ex-husband, or children's father is man enough to pay child support, please do the rest of us who do not get child support a favor, and stop complaining about it! Regardless of your relationship status with him, if this man is financially supporting those children with you, be grateful. Try maintaining those kids without that financial support, and see how different your lives would be.

I am so proud of my little women, and I am proud of myself. I credit God for giving me strength and endurance that I never knew I had. I thank God for giving me patience that I *really* never knew I had. I thank God for allowing me to see past teenage rebellion, and for allowing my teenagers to see that I'm not trying to make their lives a living hell. I'm simply trying to teach and protect them.

So, I am thankful, I am blessed, and I am ready to seize the new day...after a weeklong nap and case of some good Riesling.

At first I was going to write, "Thank God for the law because the law has saved your

life," but it's really not the law that saved you. It was God.

I fear God. I fear His wrath. I fear upsetting Him by my actions.

So, you really need to thank God for God, because my fear of Him, has saved you from

pain, torture, and permanent paralysis. I really wanted to have you dealt with.

I wish I could go back in time and understand what was so weak in my character that I

allowed your worthless existence into my life.

What goodness did I see in you that I would allow myself an attempt to bond as one with

you?

What the fuck was I thinking??????

Go ahead and live your useless life on the run. Keep running boy.

One thing I learned about you, is you are an excellent sprinter,

...but sweetheart, I run marathons.

As I sat on the ottoman massaging her terribly swollen feet and ankles, I felt her gratitude. At eighty-nine years old she was lifeless and weighed about the same. I contemplated her quality of life at that moment.

She was a bombshell in her prime. She was full of life, vigor, energy, and a whole lot of attitude. She was never the stereotypical grandmother who sat in a rocking chair knitting sweaters and sipping tea. She could absolutely throw down in the kitchen, but she was fly. She sipped red wine, rocked a mink coat, had an amazing figure, and she always had her face done and her hair did.

It just about killed me to see her immobile. Trying to get her to take four steps with assistance was torturous for her. This was a woman who jogged along side of me when I learned to ride my bike, and was a regular at the gym. She was often mistaken for my mother and I loved the shocked looks when I'd tell people that she was actually my grandmother. Damn, I hope those genes don't let me down later.

When I walked into her room earlier that day I refused to be any other way than myself. She wasn't going to see that I was hurting to see her in the condition she was in. I looked at her and said in my typical playful tone, "Grammie! What's up sexy?!" and kissed her face. The smile I received from that was priceless. Her memory had been shot for several years, but she clearly appreciated me and held my hand. That hand was so frail now. It was so hard to believe that was the same hand that kneaded the best homemade bread on the planet, or even occasionally backhanded me when I got out of line.

Despite it all, the nurses had her dressed and she looked adorable in her pink Ralph Lauren Polo and a lovely lime green and bright orange scarf around her neck. Even immobile she was jazzy. I wasn't feeling the uncombed hair so of course the diva in me had to do something. I thought a few cornrows would be slick so I hunted for a soft bristled brush, grabbed a comb for the clean parts, and went to work. I don't think she even cared about the style but I'm sure the brushing of her soft gray hair was relaxing to her as she closed her eyes and started to fall asleep. When she woke, her hair was done. It was nothing eccentric, just a little something to keep Grammie's look together.

I was hesitant to show her pictures of my daughters. I wasn't sure how she would respond. I didn't want to know if she didn't remember them. My feelings were so selfish. I wanted my regular conversations with her and I knew that wasn't going to happen. She could barely speak. My Blackberry received a picture message from Kyetra who asked me to show a particular picture to her to see if she remembered. I had to do it for my girls. I opened the file and enlarged it a bit and asked Grammie, "Do you remember this?" The photo was of her with my daughters and me. It was taken when the twins were about a year old. I really didn't expect her to smile and softly say "Yes." That was when the tears began. I messaged Kyetra back and excitedly shared that she not only remembered the photo, but also extended her hand out and asked for my phone back to look at it again.

She often asked of the time and just wanted to go back to bed so I knew our time together would be short. I vowed to visit again before I returned back home, so on that day it was easy to leave.

I took a day in between visits as re-adjusting to the Colorado altitude always takes me extra time these days. It seemed like the drive took much longer on my next visit. My mother, brother and I carried on conversations about school, sports, and weather, while Grammie sat in her throne either unresponsive or asleep. The reality of my visit started to kick in, and my conversation began to diminish.

The nurses came in and out, and a dose of morphine was administered orally for pain. There would be no more walking anywhere. The hospice nurse said that our job is to make her comfortable. My selfishness flared up again and all I could do was sit back, remain quiet, and let folks do their jobs. When the last nurse for the evening arrived, my mother and I helped her to put Grammie in her bed. That was all she wanted and I just couldn't find it in myself to be content with that.

I knew it was time to leave her, and I knew it would be the last time I saw her with breath. I could not find it in myself to leave. I was given time alone and I didn't even know what to do with it. I kneeled on the floor next to her bed and sobbed. I could only mutter "The Lord's Prayer" and ask God for the strength to get up and leave. She opened her eyes and I told her how much I loved her and that I hoped she could understand and feel the strength of what I was saying since it was flooded with tears and stuttering. She said, "I love you too. God bless you." I stroked her soft silver hair as she closed her eyes and went to sleep.

Six mornings later as the spirit of a local choir moved me, she transitioned. I thank God for that. I don't think I could have handled it any other way. I needed that spirit. My cell phone was showing several missed calls from my brother and uncles and I knew I had to accept what I didn't want to hear. My friend helped me get to my car after I collapsed and threw my phone and all I was carrying. She held me and said "You knew." I did.

When I saw her resting in her Sunday best the distress in her body was gone, the pain and frustration in her face were gone, and she had a slight grin on her lips as she held her rosary beads and her good book. Wearing the bright lime green and orange scarf that she wore when we were last together, I brushed her hair back as I did just a few days ago. It felt the same even though her body was cold. I covered her hands since she couldn't grab mine, kissed her beautiful face, and sang my girl some traveling music from one of her favorite men. "Hi-dee hi-dee hi-dee hi... ... Ho-dee ho-dee ho-dee ho!"

The lime green and orange scarf no longer smells like her. Perhaps this means her spirit is completely free. I wear it now for style of course, but mostly as a tangible token of comfort.

Yvette Williams

After the Storm

I keep looking at the spot you once claimed.

I remember how you danced, laughed, and the faces we made at each other

I wasn't sure how I would be able to go back- knowing that you would not be there

But to this day your spot remains open

No one stands in your spot.

At first I thought it was a display of honor

Now I realize, you never left it.

For my Wendy "Sah-Rah" R.I.P.

I remember stealing appetite suppressants from the grocery store at age sixteen because

my stepfather said that he would have to pay someone to take me to my senior prom

because I was loud, dumpy, and fat.

I was only 120 pounds with a definitive curve

I ate appetite suppressants and lettuce for a week. Then I got sick.

I didn't know how to make the fat go away.

At age twenty-three, I stopped stealing appetite suppressants. And I just stopped eating.

I dropped to 100 pounds…and the fat was still there

It hasn't been as glamorous as you may think.

It's amazing how damaging words can be.

To learn that I am not what society deems as beautiful, fit, or sexy- and hear it at home

Twenty years later oh, they want it, they buy it, they attach it, they implant it,

and they look so stupid.

Screw the media, society and anyone finally validating who I am physically.

Yvette Williams

I can embrace my ass now, but it's been one hell of a responsibility.

And don't touch me.

I've been assaulted, degraded, accosted, mocked, and abused for decades.

Filling out a pair of jeans isn't criminal but some the reactions I've received truly are.

The Rock

Just check on me when you can
Accept that I'm not always the strong, Black woman, designed to be this pillar of strength for everyone.

Check on me when you can
I too get weak, frightened, and seek the company of those who do not enter my life simply to suck the life out of me.

Check on me when you can
Even a mountain becomes weak after it has been chipped at for decades.
Feet, picks, hands, equipment take its toll on the establishment steadfast on its base while serving as the foundation for all who simply pick and chip and take what they need

      and leave satisfied.

When others scream, I act.

When I scream, others re-act.

Check on me when you can… or can you?

Yvette Williams

A Heavy Confession

I've struggled with my weight most of my life
Illnesses, prescriptions, steroids, depression, carelessness, lack of
self-control, resentment, and anger all played a role

I've been called fat a lot
I became conditioned to being called some kind of adjective that
referred to my weight
Or my ass

To me, thick was slang for fat
Big boned
I tried claiming that once
I was being teased and had to come up with something
It didn't work

I was called "fat ass" all throughout high school and college
There were girls bigger than me
There were asses larger than mine
They even took part in mocking me
I suppose I was the chosen one

I took drastic measures to minimize my weight
And my ass
Only to learn that starvation just makes me sick
And vomit burns my vocal cords

My mother was always a slender, stunning woman
Her side of the family was slim
I always felt so uncomfortable being around them
I felt like the fat one
Like I didn't fit in

I struggled with my weight when I was a size 14
I struggled with my weight when I was a size 4
I struggle with it now

I raised young ladies with self-esteem
Far beyond what I have ever possessed
That was the best gift I could have given them
There were times when I would look at them
And not even see myself
Their beauty and frames were unlike my own at that age
I became ashamed
I didn't look how I thought their mother should

They would often ask me why I wore big clothes
I told them for comfort
I couldn't admit
I hated my body

I guess this is to say
Words can be knives that slice through the esteem of anyone
Who is in the process of evolving
The words that are placed on us intentionally or unintentionally
Affect us forever

It took me years to recover from the pain of being called fat and
fat-ass
I'm not sure that I'm fully healed

As individuals we create our own reality
Some may see it as inaccurate
That is not their place to judge
We exist based on how we feel
If we feel good, we are good

Throughout my existence, I have allowed far too many

To define my reality
I have allowed my weight to dictate my self worth and value
It became my identity
I ignored my God given talents and allowed my weight to remain
Center stage for decades

Because I was called fat

I do not know how to eliminate these scars
I do not know how to close this chapter
I do not know if either is possible

So I will do my best to begin anew

My name is Yvette... and I am beautiful.

My Attitude

I have an attitude. I have an attitude problem. My best friend says I need an attitude adjustment. And ya know I just laughed my ass off and said "So?" I love my attitude. I need my attitude. Without it I would be amongst many who have not the strength to tell others to kiss their ass, and that's a state I never wish to be in again.

This attitude that so many refer to is so funny to me. I've been called selfish, evil, rude, one-sided, stuck-up, bitch, insensitive, and all kinds of shit, but when I was on the edge of the world ready to toss in the towel, where were these people then? When I was broke down, where were they? When I was weak and believed God Himself couldn't help me, even though He did, where were these same shit talking people? So I take all those names -every last one of them and shove them straight down the sweaty throats of the bastards that actually had the nerve to spit 'em out. It is my attitude that keeps me strong. The words "so," "and," "whatever," and "kiss my ass" have been saving graces to my self-esteem, and my success. Of course I have my weaknesses. My biggest weakness just may be my attitude. So?

Honestly, I used to have a dangerous inferiority complex. I used to ask myself "Who are you?' And I would always answer back "I don't know." But I learned. And it took crashing and burning and witnessing the fire of hell first hand. It took lost love, wasted time, and circumstantial evidence. It also took thirty-five years. Therefore, I feel justified in telling anyone who thinks they have one up on me in terms of me to kiss my ass. Don't you?

I get called a whore from jealous broads, I'm accused of sleeping with men I don't even know, I'm hated by women who want my status without the work I put into it, I'm forever ragged on about aesthetic trivial bullshit, and I'm constantly reminded that

I'm not the accepted standard of American beauty. What do I do? Cry? Starve? Nah, I toss my hands up in the air and give you the greatest quote my dear mother gave me. "Fuck 'em all."

Yes, I have an attitude and I love my attitude and maybe one day if not already you'll finally relate and say to yourself "Wow. That was one tough lady." And I'll smile from wherever I am and say, "You damn right."

Slow Down

I've had my share of casual affairs I need
Compassion and a little more honesty
I think it's time I made you aware of my needs

Don't go telling me bout the love you need
Slow down cause if you want this affair to stay
Just hold on to the temporary way we feel now

Take your time let's do this right

Slow down, don't want to lose control
Slow down, let nature take its toll
Slow down, I want to take my time
Let my passion be your guide, cause I want to let you inside

I want a stronger love that will endure- so strong
The test of time I don't want to play no more
Some respect gives so much more

Take your time you'll see, boy stop rushing me
I know just you want I'll do you right
If it's meant to be
It will happen naturally

I'll be yours soon enough in time

Slow down, don't want to lose control
Slow down, let nature take its toll
Slow down, I want to take my time
Let my passion be your guide, cause I want to let you inside

I'll be yours soon enough in time.

You Are Everything

I still feel the kiss you left with me
The way you touched my face and told me
"Don't cry baby."

I'm walking away crying in the rain
My smile won't be the same without
Your love here with me

Why does love have to be so damned lonely
I can't understand why circumstances plague me
Why must I prove my love ten times over
All I want is to be closer, closer

You are everything that I need in my life
Sun in my sky and the stars in my night
Air that I need to survive
Without you in my life I would die without you

The late nights when these tears burn down my face
Restless man, I need you do you feel me reaching
You can't imagine what I'm going through
I'm slowly dying I just want to be close to you

Why does love have to be so damned lonely
I can't understand why circumstances plague me
Why must I prove my love ten times over
All I want is to be closer, closer

You are everything that I need in my life
Sun in my sky and the stars in my night
Air that I need to survive
Without you in my life I would die without you

Yvette Williams

You are the sun in my sky
You are the starts in my night
You are the air that I need
     To survive

Can't Resist

I want him to
Lay his body next to mine
Let his love shine through
Hold me close throughout the night
I've never been
So in love like this before
Baby please don't stop
Giving me more

I need a man who loves me he keeps me so satisfied
And when the going gets rough he remains right by my side
He's all the man I've wanted he's all the man that I need
I know I can't resist the way
He loves me.

I want him to
Love me down from head to toe
In his special ways
Take me high, don't let me go
He gives to me
More love than I've ever seen
Through our love he keeps on
Setting me free

I need a man who loves me he keeps me so satisfied
And when the going gets rough he remains right by my side
He's all the man I've wanted he's all the man that I need
I know I can't resist the way
He loves me.

My Inspiration (a musical tribute to the late Tito Puente)

The day you smiled at me
I felt the spirit of your soul
You made my childhood dreams come true
Again I thank you

Your legacy has lasted through
The generations of my life
Your rhythm lifts my spirits high
My inspiration

Your music I'll never let go
How much you're loved you'll never know
Oye de mi Guaguancó
Is in my soul and everlasting

And now I'm missing you
These memories are all I have
I'll always treasure
The day we "Ran Kan Kanned"

Your rhythm lives inside of me yes, you are my inspiration
And your music of my life will live forever Mambo caliente
Your rhythm lives inside of me yes, you are my inspiration
And with you no longer here my world of music es más diferente

Your rhythm lives inside of me yes, you are my inspiration
May you have a peaceful journey God be with you El Rey solamente
Your rhythm lives inside of me yes, you are my inspiration
You will always have a special place in my heart God bless Tito
Puente

Thank You

Beautiful man with your beautiful ways
Saved me from my fear of pain
And let me love again

Beautiful smile with your hand around mine
Opened up your soul for me
I'm so proud to be your queen

And you love me, the way I need
Beyond belief and I

I just want to thank you
For the love you give me
Thank you for loving me without having me
Compromise my integrity

Blessed I finally found the man of my dreams
Sacrificed to take my hand
And you love me as I am

You make me whole, embraced my soul
Love uncontrolled and I

I just want to thank you
For the love you give me
Thank you for loving me without having me
Compromise my integrity

And you love me, the way I need
Beyond belief and I thank you
You make me whole, embraced my soul
Love uncontrolled and I just want to thank you.

What Must I Do

I lost composure on the night I laid my eyes on you
I thought up schemes and anything just to get next to you
I had a plan you'd be my man and all would be all right

Somewhere in line I lost my stride and things fell to the side
And soon I also learned that time wasn't quite on my side
The mystery was killing me I had to take my chance

I can make it right, don't want to be alone tonight
Don't make me fight you for it tell me, tell me

What must a sista do- to spend some time with you
Do almost anything- just to get next to you
What must I do just to make love to you-tonight

A simple kiss that led to this I can't believe my eyes
I dedicate my body just to keep you satisfied
Look in my eyes there's no surprise I want to take you there

I must insist I can't resist you you're my fantasy
Don't want to scare you but I dare you fall in love with me
I want to know just how you flow and if you'll take me there

I can make it right, don't want to be alone tonight
Don't make me fight you for it tell me, tell me

What must a sista do- to spend some time with you
Do almost anything- just to get next to you
What must I do just to make love to you-tonight

By Myself

Got me going out my mind
Feeling like I'm wasting time
Gotta get back on my grind
I'm better off all by myself

No more fuss and fights we're through
I don't need your attitude
No more dealing with your hell
I'm better off all by myself

Didn't rush baby I thought it out realize that I can't stay in love
with these doubts
I've been thinking
There ain't no sense in continuing on, there's no trust in my heart
and the passion is gone
No more faking

Misery loves company they say
Who the hell is they- I can count the ways

Got me going out my mind
Feeling like I'm wasting time
Gotta get back on my grind
I'm better off all by myself

No more fuss and fights we're through
I don't need your attitude
No more dealing with your hell
I'm better off all by myself

Tried to be what you want me to be giving up what I had just to
keep you with me

Was about you
You were my king baby you were my star, I even held your hand
when I prayed to my God
I stayed faithful

Misery loves company they say
Who the hell is they- I can count the ways

No-no no-no forget it
You can't play my insecurities
Oh-no no-no forget it
Take that bitch, she's no better than me
No-no I don't regret it
Miss your water once your well runs dry
Oh-no no-no forget it
Bounce baby ain't no more last tries

Misery loves company they say
Who the hell is they- I can count

No trials no time I ain't crying
Pack up move on with your lying
Ain't wasting no more time
I'm gonna take myself from you

No drama ain't being catty
Just better off by my dammy
Don't even waste your time
Trying to get me back baby

I only gave you my lovin'
Reciprocated with nothin'
You never had my back
Although I gave myself to you

Can't even look into my eyes man
We're at the point of demise and
You weren't worth a damn
How was I justifying you

Got me going out my mind
Feeling like I'm wasting time
Gotta get back on my grind
I'm better off all by myself

No more fuss and fights we're through
I don't need your attitude
No more dealing with your hell
I'm better off all by myself

Yvette Williams

Promises

Time and time again I'd give my heart to someone new without
receiving
My just due can't understand what is so hard in giving back to you
what's given

It always showed the lies you told
Communication could not hold
The fairy tales I dreamed of so
It broke me down you never loved me

Hope was fading dreams were shattered
My love for you didn't matter
My whole world revolved around my own illusion

How could love be so blind

Another broken heart another absent minded dream
Too many wasted nights and I can't shed no more tears
Don't bother asking me cause the love is no longer there
I won't let you bring me down no more- keep on moving

All the same I took the blame of being wrong through all
misunderstands
All I needed was some time with you I got accused of acting too
demanding

I can't believe what I am hearing
Cold as ice not even caring
Real love I thought we were sharing
All disguised by bad intentions

While I was giving you were taking
Ones I loved were trying to make a
Fool of me and all I do without a reason

Can real love still be found

Another broken heart another absent minded dream
Too many wasted nights and I can't shed no more tears
Don't bother asking me cause the love is no longer there
I won't let you bring me down no more- keep on moving

Your absent minded lies you can keep them
No apologies don't want to hear them
I took your pain and suffering but babe
You can't destroy my pride

Don't give me no words if you don't mean them
Thought you loved me guess that I was dreaming
I lived a life of fantasy and dreams
Your love was just a lie

Kitty Litter

I tried my best to make you happy
You stripped my soul completely
What in the hell was the matter with you
Trying to compete with me but now I'm through

If you're such a man why don't you stand your ground
Pissed off at myself for staying around
But now it's on and the rumors are true
I'm coming up, coming out with or without you

Oh no- shit's hit the fan now
Hell no- it's ridiculous
Oh no- I can't believe how
Hell no- I justified your bullshit

I bled for you cried over you, I damn near almost died for you
I only asked you to be near, you turned your back and disappeared
Comforted you through all your fears
You sold me out, I dried your tears
And I ain't bitter in case you figured, I'll never be your kitty litter
Bitch nigga

You tried your best to keep a sista down
But now it's my turn to flip it around
What in the hell was you thinking about
Got tired of your shiftless ass and I stepped out

Can't be around you disgrace my race
I still get sick at the sight of your face
Say what you want you was nothing but mouth
You want to call me a bitch but punk who's the bitch now

My Testimony

Looking back I finally see
The changes that created me
A lonely life with few who knew my dreams, my soul, my loves
Once hated everything about myself
Danced with the devil in the fires of hell
Wishing somebody would please understand me

But I've learned to know myself
I appreciate my help
I don't need validation from you
To do what I gotta do

After all is said and done my head is up high
Who are you to judge me you ain't lived my life
Believe what you want to believe my life has been a testimony
Struggling to find the love inside of me

Screams of pain nobody hears
Suicidal tendencies
My innocence taken away
I cried I lay confused that day

Men I thought were of my dreams
Never would commit to me
Begging for simplicity
What's so wrong with loving me

Gave myself til none was left
Lost my mind and self respect
When death was all I cared about
My God He heard me crying out

After all is said and done my head is up high
Who are you to judge me you ain't lived my life
Believe what you want to believe my life has been a testimony
Struggling to find the love inside of me

My God, I thank you. (for I know I have kept you busy)

Printed in Great Britain
by Amazon.co.uk, Ltd.,
Marston Gate.